A BRIEF INTRODUCTION TO VEDIC SCIENCE

DR. JAGADEESH PILLAI

Copyright © Dr. Jagadeesh Pillai
All Rights Reserved.

Contents

Prayer

GururBrahma GururVishnu GururDevo Maheshwaraha

Guru Saakshaat ParaBrahma Tasmai Sri Gurave Namaha

Acknowledgements

INSPIRATION TO WRITE THIS BOOK

All Credit Goes to

My Guru

Dr. N. Gopalakrishnan

Director – IISH
Scientist (Retd) , CSIR

M.Sc. (Pharm); M.Sc. (Chem.);
M.A. (Soc.); Ph.D (Bio); D.Lit

www.iish.org | E-MAIL : iishservice1@gmail.com

Indian Institute of Scientific Heritage

National Heritage Center, Mazhuvanchery, Eranellur,
Trissur 680 501

About The Author

Dr. Jagadeesh Pillai a voracious reader, Four Times Guinness World Record holder, writer, and true research scholar was born in Varanasi, the abode of Lord Shiva. He is Ph.D. in Vedic Science. He is a multi-faceted polymath with innate qualities, creative ideas and many remarkable achievements. Although his roots extend back to "Gods own Country"(Kerala), the residents of Varanasi feel proud of him and adore him as a child of Varanasi who caters to every individual in need without any expectations. A deep study into his profile reflects that he has added so many feathers to his cap which makes him quite unique. He is a four times Guinness Book of World Records Holder in the following subjects :

"Script to Screen" which he achieved by producing and directing a state of art animation film within the shortest time possible by breaking the earlier set record by Canadians. There are many national and international Awards and Recognitions to his credit.

Longest Line of Post Cards which he has done on the occasion of 163 years of Indian Postal Day by 16300 post cards. The event was also connected with a questionnaire about Indian Flag.

Largest Poster Awareness Campaign – This was achieved by designing an awareness campaign on the subject "Beti Bachao – Beti Padhao".

Largest Envelop – Towards tribute to Prime Minister's initiative 'Make in India' – he has created about 4000 sq meter envelop using waste papers.

Attempted by lighting 70000 candles on a 210 kg cake to celebrate the 70th Indian Independence day recorded in World Records India.

Attempted a documentary on Dhamek Stupa of Sarnath dubbing in 17 languages, result is waiting from Guinness World Records.

He is versatile in Gita teaching. The young generation is fond of his Gita teaching and he has changed the life of many young through his continued motivational boost up and teachings.

He has composed and sung Gayatri Mantra in 1000 different tunes.

He has composed and sung Hanuman Chalisa in 108 different tunes.

He has composed and sung hundreds of Sanskrit Bhajans, Patriotic songs, etc.

He has written and directed so many short films and documentaries for awareness campaigns.

He has done voluntary services to UP Police and Kerala Police to spread awareness campaigns on the various issue through videos and photography.

He is on the path of authoring thousands of books on Indian culture, Indian Temples, and the life of extraordinary people.

It is hard to believe that he has produced and directed more than 100 Documentaries on a particular city (Varanasi) which is done by a single person.

He has helped and guided more than 25 boys and girls to achieve world records through various creative and innovative methods.

A multifaceted person who can apply the best of his intellect using the God-given blessings which have been showered upon every human being granting them an immense capacity to learn, experience, and experiment with many things and do wonders in this world of discrimination and disparities.

He is a teacher and a student at the same time who always learns every day and teaches every day. As a master, his weakness was that he never sticks to a particular subject. Perhaps this weakness gives him the strength to master any area which he came across.

Each of his days dawned with learning a new topic and he spend most of his time experimenting and researching it.

He is also a selfless social activist and a motivational speaker.

His life was full of struggle, ups and downs, and failures. But he never gave up and faced all his trials and tribulations full of confidence. Today he is a successful young man with a lot of enthusiasm and rich life experience.

He has sung full Ram Charita Manas 51 hours audio by his own composition. He has also sung the whole Bhagavad-Gita in his own composition with a rhythmic background.

He has also sung "Lokah Samastha Sukhino Bhavantu" in 50 different languages.

Currently working on a detailed and scientific study on Veda, Upanishad, Puranas, Bhagavad Gita, etc.

Currently, he is the Hon' Chancellor of 'Eurasia Digital University'.

Awards

ABOUT THE AUTHOR

Four Times Guinness World Records

Winner of Mahatma Gandhi Vishwa Shanti Puraskar

Mahatma Gandhi Global Peace Ambassador
Kashi Ratna Award

Dr. APJ Abdul Kalam Motivational Person of the Year 2017

Mother Teresa Award

Indira Gandhi Priyadarshini Award

Bharat Vikas Ratna Award

Udyog Ratna Award

Vigyan Prasar Award

Poorvanchal Ratn Samman

Dr. Jagadeesh Pillai is a teacher of Vedic Science, Bhagavad Gita etc. Apart from this, he is also a Writer, Winger, Film Maker, Gemologist, Astro-Vastu Consultant, World Record Consultant, Pranic Healer, Spiritual Counsellor, Tarot Card reader etc.

He is the chairman of All India Malayali Association, Uttar Pradesh and also the National Secretary of 'Culture and Heritage' of the Indian Human Rights Association.

Preface

What is Vedic Science? Most people especially even in India itself have asked this question to me. For them, Vedas and other Vedic literature are just for prayer and God-worshipping for wish fulfilment. But they are unaware of the hidden scientific and psychological benefits behind it. Each and every ritual performed by Brahmins or priests in a temple has scientific/logical reasons. In ancient times, the temples are created for psychological healing. In Santana Dharma it is believed, maintained, and followed to heal always the psychological bodies for not to attract any diseases. But nowadays diseases are everywhere and treat them once it is diagnosed.

This gives a Brief Introduction about Vedic Science.

Dr. Jagadeesh PIllai

CHAPTER ONE

INTRODUCTION TO VEDIC SCIENCE

What is Vedic Science? Most people especially even in India itself have asked this question to me. For them, Vedas and other Vedic literature are just for prayer and God-worshipping for wish fulfilment. But they are unaware of the hidden scientific and psychological benefits behind it. Each and every ritual performed by Brahmins or priests in a temple has scientific/logical reasons. In ancient times, the temples are created for psychological healing. In Santana Dharma it is believed, maintained, and followed to heal always the psychological bodies for not to attract any diseases. But nowadays diseases are everywhere and treat them once it is diagnosed.

We can easily understand Science and Spirituality exists together from the following verse from Ishavasyo Upanishad (Verses 11):

वद्यिां च अवद्यिां च यस्तद्वेदोभयं सह ।
अवद्यिया मृत्युं तीर्त्वा वद्यियामृतमश्नुतं ।।

Vidhyam cha avidyam cha yastat Vedobhayam saha

Avidyaya-mrityum teertwa Vidhyayaamrutamashnute

This is the foundation of Indian knowledge

There are 2 types of knowledge, one is known as **Vidhya** and the other one is **Avidhya.**

Eternal, Experienceable and Spiritual knowledge is Vidhya

External, experimental, and Scientific knowledge is Avidhya

External, experimental, and Scientific knowledge is Avidhya

Use the scientific knowledge for overcoming the problems in our life.

Eternal, Experienceable and Spiritual knowledge is Vidhya

Use the Vidhya, the spiritual knowledge for attaining immortality or permanent peace.

So what we did here is utilized the scientific knowledge for solving the day to day problems in our life and and use the spiritual knowledge for attaining immortality or permanent peace.

One of the spiritual knowledge is yoga to attain healthy and peaceful life.

So we have got 2 types of knowledge. Remember vidhya and avidya. Again I will go one more step.

Vidha has been divided again into two lines :
Pure Spirituality and Applied Spirituality.

Avidhya is also divided into two lines :
Pure Science and Applied Science.

Both spirituality and science are mixed in our Vedic knowledge and culture. When we know the scientificity of every Vedic knowledge, culture, rituals etc. and start using it in life, then the real fruit of every knowledge or wisdom will be attained and satisfied, otherwise, it will remain as a meaningless ritual. The youth is running away from Vedic culture because of their ignorance of the science and logic in Vedic Culture.

The way to understand the scientism of Vedic knowledge through examples :

Example – 1

Praying to God immediately after waking up in the morning.
It is said that we should wake up in the morning, sit on the bed, as soon as we open our eyes, fold our two hands together, then open our hands and look in the hands and pray that :

कराग्रेवसतेलक्ष्मीकरमध्येसरस्वती।

करमूलेतुगोविन्दप्रभातेकरदर्शनम्।।

Maa Lakshmi resides in the forearm of the hands.

Maa Saraswati resides in the middle.

Maa Gauri should reside in the root i.e. the lower part.

Performing this prayer is a spiritual activity, but not many people know about the science behind this prayer.

What is Scientology?

When we wake up in the morning, sitting on the bed and praying the name of God is a good thing, but there is also a scientific hidden knowledge behind it. The heart also remains calm while sleeping at night. But when we wake up early in the morning on someone's call or for any other reason, the chances of having a heart attack are high because the calm heart has to work too fast than normal. When we get up and move in a high speed, the blood flow to the heart increases. It has been seen in research around the world that most of the heart attacks have happened in the morning while getting up so fast or while lying on the bed so fast.

Therefore, the science behind reciting this mantra is that when we wake up in the morning, sit on the bed for at least 3 seconds and then get up comfortably, so that the heart gets a chance to work comfortably.

Second example:

After waking up in the morning, salutations to mother earth with a mantra.

समुद्रवसनेदेवपिर्वतस्तनमण्डलो
विष्णुपत्ननिमस्तुभ्यंपादस्पर्शंक्षमस्वमो।

Meaning: O Bhumi Devi, who wears the clothes of the sea, has mountain-like breasts and is the wife of Lord Shri Vishnu! I greet you, Forgive me for touching your feet.

It is not that only our feet live on the earth, but we are living on the earth in its entirety. Apart from keeping feet, many wrong and dirty things are also done on earth. Yet in our Sanatan Dharma, because of seeing the divinity in everything, we also bow down to Mother Earth in this way.

What is the science behind this?

When we sleep by changing sides at night, magnetic static electricity is generated around our body which is negative for our body. If we put our feet on the ground immediately in the morning, then the pure electric current inside our body (which is useful for our healthy body for day-to-day life), becomes earth in the ground and a negative magnetic electric current enters inside the body.

When we touch the earth with our hands on the pretext of praying, then the negative magnetic electric current gets earthed in the earth and the pure electric current inside our body remains as it is. By doing this daily, we can work the whole day without getting tired from the morning to evening and can also get rid of many diseases.

Similarly, behind every mantra or spiritual or Vedic thing, there is a scientific hidden truth behind it, but we are ignorant about it. Having both spiritual and scientific knowledge will help us to understand everything in nature.

CHAPTER TWO

VEDAS

Veda means knowledge. The collection of knowledge acquired by our sages through their divine vision are there in the Vedas. The other meaning of Veda is - to be, to know, to think and to receive. Through the Vedas, the knowledge or understanding of the existence of Dharma, Artha, Kama and Moksha in the form of Purushartha is obtained. Veda is from time immemorial; Veda is from the beginning of creation. There is no definite opinion about the author of the Vedas.

Vedas tell the path of progress and it teaches how to avoid the ill-effects of misdeeds.

There are other words in the meaning of Veda which are used such as:

Shruti, Nigam, Aagama, Trayi, Chandas, Amnaya, Swadhyaya.
   SHRUTI

The Guru used to teach the Veda Mantras to the disciple by the traditional method and the disciple used to memorize the Mantras by listening to them. The disciples used to pay special attention to the correct vowel and correct pronunciation while memorizing the mantras. Special emphasis was given to ensure that there should be no errors related to vowels and pronunciation while remembrance of the mantras.

NIGAM

The Vedas are called Nigams because of their relevant, serious meaning and intention. Nigam means meaningful or one who gives knowledge of meaning.

AGAMA

The word Agama is used for Vedas and Shastras.

TRAYI

Trayi means three Vedas, Rigved, Yajurved and Sama Veda. Atharvaveda also comes under the TRAYI (Mimamsa Sutra 2.1.35-37).

CHANDAS

The meaning of verse is to cover or to cover. Methodical compositions are called verses. In the second meaning, one's sentiments are systematically bound in verse, that is called chhand.

AAMNAYA

Aamnaya means the knower of the four Vedas. Aamnaya emphasizes on practicing the Vedas every day.

SWAADHYAYA (STUDY ABOUT SELF)

The word Swadhyaya emphasizes on contemplation and always practice about the Self. Do not indulge in the study and propagation of Vedas (Taitti. Upa. 01.11.1)

CHAPTER THREE

IMPORTANCE OF VEDAS

The cornerstone of Aryadharma is the Vedas. Vedas are the only means to know and understand Dharma (Duties). All the duties of human beings are directed in the Vedas. The goal of life is salvation, doing work with a selfless spiritVedas are considered important in many respects such as:

1.Religious Significance

2. Classical Significance

3. Importance of Code of Conduct

4. Social Significance

5. Economic Importance

6. Scientific Elements

7. Poetic and Literary Significance

8. Political Significance

9. Linguistic Significance

10. Historical importance etc.

Daily study of Vedas describes the attainment of life, opulence, prosperity, food etc.

Division of Vedic Literature

For convenience, the Vedic literature is divided into the following four parts:

1. Samhitas of the Vedas

2. Brahmana texts

3. Aranyaka Granth

4. Upanishads

Samhitas of the Vedas - This Samhita is four: Rigveda Samhita, Yajurveda Samhita, Samaveda Samhita and Atharvaveda Samhita. (Mantra part is called Samhita).

Brahmana texts - Vedas and Brahmana texts come under rituals. The process of performing various types of yagyas is done through rituals. The information of all the mantras related to the rituals for the sacrifice is described in detail in the BBrahmanatext.

Aranyaka texts and 4. Upanishads - Aranyaka texts and Upanishads come under the Gyankand (wisdom sector). The spiritual and philosophical explanation of Yagya's has been given in Aranyaka Granth. The creation of the Upanishads is considered by this spiritual interpretation. They describe Brahma, Paramatma, Prakriti, Jiva, Moksha, etc.

Vedanga – (Detailed information is available in the next chapter) - The parts of Veda are called Vedanga.

CHAPTER FOUR

BRIEF ABOUT FOUR VEDAS

Rigveda:

The oldest and first Veda. The basic theme of Rigveda is 'Knowledge' and the praise of God etc. are described and the number of mantras is 10627.

Yajurveda:

In this Veda, there is a description of the process of work and sacrifice or it can be said that there is a description of action and dedication. It has a total of 1975 Gadyatik (prose) Mantras.

Samaveda:

The subject of Samaveda is worship and musical dedications through mantras are described. It has a total of 1875 musical chants.

Atharvaveda:

In Atharvaveda, the subject of religion, health and sacrifice etc. are described. This Veda contains Kavitamayi Mantra whose number is 5977.

CHAPTER FIVE

GENERAL INTRODUCTION TO VEDIC LITERATURE

Vedic literature gives the sense of knowledge and wisdom. In order to understand the Vedic literature easily, it has been divided into four parts:-

Samhitas of Vedas, Brahmanas, Aranyakas and Upanishads. Along with these four parts, Vedangas are also divided under Vedic literature. Along with these, it is very necessary to study many texts like Pratishakhya, Dharmashastra, etc. and the sub-Vedas of the four Vedas for the complete study of the Vedas.

Therefore, Vedic literature is considered to be the world's oldest source for understanding Hinduism. The Vedic literature was received by the sages only through the Shravan (listening) tradition.

CHAPTER SIX

VEDIC SAMHITAS

The main parts of the mantras of the Vedas are called Samhitas. The word 'Samhita' means collection. Samhitas are those parts of mantras that are specifically studied (chanted) every day. The description of how to praise the God is found in Samhitas. In the text of the Samhitas, special emphasis is given to letters, vowels, characters etc., Their language is Vedic Sanskrit. The four Vedas are called the four Samhitas and it has four different branches also.

Here the general introduction of the four Vedas or four Samhitas is being given in a nutshell which is as follows:

(1) RIGVED SAMHITA

(2) YAJURVED SAMHITA

(3) SAMVED SAMHITA

(4) ATHARVAVED SAMHITA

RIGVED SAMHTA (1800-1100 BC)

The meaning of Rik or Richa is 'Mantra for praise of

Divine'. In Rigveda, various deities are praised and invoked by these mantras.

All Indian and Western scholars consider Rigveda to be the oldest text of the world. Rigveda is considered to be the most important and revered of the four Vedas. The Rigveda is the oldest and the largest of the four Vedas in terms of language and verses.

***

YAJURVED SAMHITA (7000-1500 BC)

The word Yajurveda is also called Yajus or Yaju: because the name Yajurveda is derived from the name Yajus.

(Yajus + Veda = Yajurveda) – Yaja means 'surrender'.
The offering of substances (such as fuel, ghee, etc.), yoga, karma (service, tarpan), sense control, shraadh etc. is called the act of surrender. It contains the description of 3988 mantras. Mantras related to Yagya are called Yajus or the mantras with which Yagya is performed are called Yajus. Yajurveda is directly related to the rituals of sacrifices, hence it is also called 'Adhvaryuveda (अध्वर्युवेद) '. The social and religious life of the Yajurveda Aryans and the Varna system, Varnashrama etc. have been highlighted.

Yajurveda has a collection of mantras for yagya to organize rituals of Vedic period religion. It describes about many ritualistic sacrifices like Agnihotra, Ashwamedha, Vajapeya, Somayyagya, Rajasuya, Agnichana. Yajurveda has two branches, one is Shukla Yajurveda and the other is Krishna Yajurveda.

1. Shukla Yajurveda :- (Aditya Sampradaya)

This Shukla branch of Yajurveda is prevalent in North India. Shukla Yajurveda has a purely hymnical part related to Yagyas, it does not have explanation, description and appropriative part. Therefore, these mantras are read as it is in Yagyas. Due to pure and refined, it is called Shukla Yajurveda. On this basis, Brahmins, who are the patrons of Shukla Yajurveda, have been named "Shukla".

2. Krishna Yajurveda :- (Brahma Sampradaya)

This Krishna branch of Yajurveda is prevalent in South India. In Krishna Yajurveda, along with the mantras, the part of interpretation and appropriation is also mixed. Therefore it is called Krishna (unclean or mixed) Yajurveda. On this basis, the Brahmins of Krishna Yajurveda have been given the name "Mishra".

SAMVED SAMHITA

Saam or Sama means the mantra is like Poems or Songs. When Mantras are rendered in the form of Songs, it is called Sama. Sa (Richa) + Aam (Singing) = Saam (Saam). The number of mantras in Samaveda is 1875. Samaveda Chanting is predominant, at the time of Yagya or Havan or ritual. Shri Krishna gave the highest place to Samaveda in the Gita and considered Samaveda to be the form of God. The Yagya is not complete without the samagan and the one who knows the Samaveda will be able to know the secrets of the Veda.

By the methodical chanting of various mantras of Samaveda, ill free health, wish fulfilment etc. can be attained. Samaveda is Triveni consisting of three Yogas; Jnana Yoga, Karma Yoga, and Bhakti Yoga. Modern scholars have also accepted this fact from Samaveda itself has all the musical and performing arts ingredients like swar, rhythms, verses, speed, vocal therapy, raga, dance postures and expressions etc.

Modern scientists have now come to know about many such truths, which are described in the mantras of Samaveda, such as the rays of the sun merging in the moon's circle and illuminating.

The one who performs the music is called 'Samag'. With a pure heart, samagan (Singing of Samaveda Mantras) attracts all the gods. Samagan is the best way to praise God and to please the Gods. The swaras have already been described in the Samaveda, which in modern Hindustani music is known as sa-re-ga-ma-pa-dha-ni. In the Vedic period, many instruments like Veena, Dundabhi, Turabh, Nadi, Bankura etc. have been specially mentioned in the Mantras of Samaveda.

ATHARVAVEDA SAMHITA (7000- 500 BC)

Atharvaveda or Atharvan is one and the same. Ath + Arvak = Atharva. The Veda in which the knowledge of seeing the soul within oneself is preached is Atharvaveda. Atharvaveda is believed to be related to yoga sadhana, attainment of Brahman and cessation of mind. In Atharvaveda, there are descriptions of 6000 hymns and there is an extension of mantras of praise of gods, medicine, science and philosophy etc.

Atharva Veda is also called Brahma Veda and contains many mantras related to Brahma worship. From the point of view of Ayurveda, this Veda is very important because in it Ayurvedic medicine systems have been described in many ways. Innumerable herbs, treatment of serious diseases, surgery, discussion of diseases arising from worms, remedies to remove death, botany, reproductive science, salvation, astronomy and geography etc. can be treated through Atharvaveda.

Atharvaveda comes in the last i.e. fourth place among the four Vedas. This is a later Veda but the most important because this is the Brahma Veda, where there is Brahma, and there is Atharva. This Veda is comprehensive and it is not limited to rituals only, but is described in many contexts like spiritual, philosophical, social, economic, education and science, Abhichara Karma (rituals done with negative intentions to harm somebody), Ayurveda etc. The Atharvaveda is like the ocean in Gagar.

The five sub-Vedas of Atharvaveda, in which (1) Sarpaveda, (2) Pishcha Veda, (3) Asurveda (4) History Veda (5) Purana Veda are mentioned.

CHAPTER SEVEN

VEDANG

The part of Veda is called Vedanga. Helpful elements are obtained by Vedanga to know the real meaning of Vedas and the mystery contained in Vedas.

These Vedangas are of 6 types - Education, Kalpa, Grammar, Astrology, Verses, Nirukta.

How to pronounce the words correctly, for this 'Shiksha Granth' was composed.

Etymology of the words - what is the meaning of the word? What is the sublime vowel? for this, the book 'Grammar and Pratisakhya' was composed.

In the Vedas, 'Chhand' was composed for the composition and pronunciation of verses.

How are words formed? What is its original meaning? What is the definitional meaning? for this knowledge 'Nirukta or Nirvachan Shastra' was composed.

When is the Yagya? When is the auspicious time? When is the full moon day? - 'Astrology' was composed for the purpose of knowledge.

Each Yagya method, the material required for the Yagya, which mantra should be read in the Yagya? How many pundits are there to recite the mantra? The 'Kalpa Granth' was composed for many small and big directions like the size, shape, etc. of the altar.

Therefore, it is emphasized to pronounce the mantra correctly with the correct shruti. If there is even a slight error in the vowel, character, or meaning, then it gives the opposite effect. Therefore, Vedanga is essential for a clear knowledge of the vowels and meanings of the Vedas. These six Vedangas are described as the six parts of the Veda Purush.

1. Feet of Veda Purush - Verse

2. Hands of Veda Purush - Kalpa

3. Face of Veda Purush - Grammar

4. Nose of Veda Purush - Education

5. Ears of Veda Purush - Nirukta

6. Eye of Veda Purusha – Astrology

1. Education (Shiksha) - (Nose of Veda Purush)

In which the correct pronunciation of vowels and letters etc. are taught, it is called shiksha. How many vowels are there and how to pronounce which vowel, what is the place of pronunciation of varna, in what form and how many efforts are there, etc. have been described in shiksha. In shiksha, these six things are important: Varna, Swar, meter, Force, Sama and Antaap. There are 35 education texts available in which the recitation of mantras etc. has been described in detail.

In some "Shiksha Sutras" there are Shikshasutras of Apishali, Panini and Chandragomi and many important points related to phonology are available in it.

2. Grammar - (Ved Purush's mouth)

Grammar is said to be the mouth of the Vedas. Grammar was created to know the purpose of Vedas and the real knowledge of words.

3. Nirukta - (Ear of the Veda Purusha)

Nirukta is called the soul of Vedas. The work of Nirukta is to provide knowledge of the root form of the word, to explain the nature of the suffix, to explain the synonyms and non-meaning words, etc. It is also called the ear of the Veda Purush.

4. Jyotish - (Eye of Veda Purush)

Jyotish Veda is also called the Eye of Purusha because it provides guidance for Yagya etc. Astrology is called Kaal Gyan Shastra or a combination of both Kal Vigyan and Astrology. Astrology is the science that tells the motion of celestial objects like stars, sun, moon, planets, etc. Just as the peacock's crest and the snake's gem are in the topmost place of the head, similarly mathematics and astrology are in the topmost place in the whole of Vedanga.

For the knowledge of the fixed period of Jyotish Yagya etc. i.e. in which period one should or should not perform the Yagya etc., it is very necessary to have the knowledge of astrology.

5. Kalpa - (Hand of Veda Purush)

The text in which the entire law and order of small and big yagyas described in the Vedas have been described is called Kalpa Granth. Kalpa is also called the hand of Veda Purush. In the Kalpasutra, clear instructions have been given about the whole method from the beginning to the end of the Yagya, such as - according to which order the work is to be done in the yagya, what is the work of each pandit, by which method the mantra is to be used, etc.

6. Chhand - (Feet of Veda Purush)

The meaning of the chhand is that the cover is made of metal. The verse envelops the emotion and gives it a collective form, due to which the verse becomes lyrical and legible. Chhand is considered to be the foot of the Veda Purush, which provides stability, just as the foot provides stability to our body. These verses are the cover of the Vedas and it is through the verses that the knowledge of the composition of Gayatri etc.

CHAPTER EIGHT

LOGIC BEHIND VEDIC CULTURE

AGNIHOTRA

Agnihotra is a Vedic sacrifice, which is described in Yajurveda. This is called the daily Vedic Yagya. Agnihotra is done by offering hawan samagries to the divine fire (homa kundam). In the Vedic period, there was a custom of making an altar of sacrifice according to the Shulvasutra i.e. geometry by bringing Samidha from the forest to perform the Yagya.

It is said that if Agnihotra is performed with Gayatri Mantra or Tryambakam Mantra in our homes for 20 minutes, then for 24 hours a protective shield is formed around us, due to which any negative element does not affect us.

World's first place in Bhopal, India, where Agnihotra has been adopted on a large scale which was started by Mr. Mo Jio Poddar. After this, in America, Chile, Poland and West Germany, Agnihotra is performed to make the city pollution free.

The materials required for Agnihotra are very less:

A copper vessel that is 6"x6"x6"

Dried Cow Dung Cakes

Pure Ghee

Rice

Black Sesame

Sunrise and sunset also have a significance for Agnihotra.

In the morning and evening, the golden rays of the sun fall obliquely, in which many medicinal properties are contained.

YAGYA KUND

In the Vedas, there is a description of the shape of the Yagya altar, especially in the shape of a circle, quadrilateral, and crescent. According to the Vedic Agama, there are ten types of Yagya Kunds, and these ten types of Yagya Kunds are considered to be symbols of ten types of figures, some of them are written about:

Informer Yagyakund - Peace Information

Arlivrit Yagyakund - To be blessed

Triveni Loan

Yagyakund - attainment of happiness and prosperity

Businessman Yagyakund - Going for business work

Eight Kiyagakunda - Spiritual power and accomplishment

Nakin Yagyakund - freedom from chanting or traveling of great mantras.

Pollution-free by Yagyas

The environment can be kept safe by yajna, earlier yagyas were performed in all villages and homes, so that neither drought nor epidemic was seen in that area. But gradually we are becoming modern and we are forgetting the Vedic tradition, neither do Yagya nor do we go to any Yagya.

Perhaps this is the reason why we are getting stricken with physical and mental suffering. The environment around us is slowly getting polluted, many are suffering from pollution.

Yagya smoke in air pollution

Divine herbs and plants are used in the Yagyas and the substances used in the Yagyas have the power to purify the environment. Due to these fumes, germs are destroyed and humans remain healthy, along with the smoke of these sacrifices, there is rain, which is considered beneficial for agriculture and the most important thing is that air pollution is less and the purification of the environment is more.

Yagya mantras in noise pollution

The chanting of the right mantras causes vibrations which purifies the whole environment, their effect falls on both the body and the mind of the human being. Noise pollution is reduced due to the waves emanating from the chanting of the mantra.

Ashes of Yagya in Soil Pollution

Barren land can also be made fertile from the ashes left after the yajna. Many times when the seeds are not able to germinate, the seeds are soaked in the ashes of the Yagya and left for 24 hours and the ash is sprinkled in the fields, which increases the fertility of the soil. Whatever crops were grown in such soils were found to be chemical free and flourishing in large quantities.

Ashes of Yagya in water pollution

This experiment has been seen in many Gurukuls that the ashes of the Yagya were spread in a container and a fine mesh was placed at the bottom, and dirty water was poured into the container. When the water filtered out from the ashes performed in the yajna, it was tested and found to be many times purer than the water of Bisleri (Mineral Water).

CHAPTER NINE

MANTRA HEALING

'Mantra Healing' means that one who comes under the shelter of spiritual medicine definitely becomes free from troubles or diseases. Sattvikata (purity) has been considered a very important method for the worship of mantras. In this, care has to be taken of the purification of the place and the sage. Mantra healing is also pure spirituality.

The body is mortal but the mantra is immortal. The effect of mantras extends to the heart-mind, and soul. When chanting mantras, listening to their sound with the ears, then every hair and body experiences immense power and peace. Why? Because in mantras lies the power of the universe.

Effect of Mantras

The basis of the effect of the iconic idol in the temple is the mantra itself because, without mantra accomplishment, the instrument or the idol does not give its effect. Your speech, your body, and your thoughts make everyone effective. Therefore, adding 'healing' to mantras made it omnipotent.

In fact, 'healing' is an English word which means to provide a healthy mind and healthy body. Many people say that this word should be changed because many do not understand its meaning. But instead of focusing on the word, we should focus on its power and its function. After all, whatever the word, the work should be energetic and fulfilling.

According Mantra Doctor Mr. to Sanjay Lodha Jain, when a particular person is made to sit or lie down in the healing chamber for 'Mantra Healing', then after examining, the internal power of his body can be examined by dowsing and we can understand how mantra power help him to heal better.

'Mantra Healing' and 'Dowsing Astrology' are synonyms of each other. Where possibilities are explored with Dowsing Astrology, their solutions are found, whereas all solutions are done with Mantra Healing. In the same way, God is one and His forms are many.

Mantra therapy is literally sound wave therapy. Sounds are generated from the recitation of mantra and go in the form of waves in the atmosphere (upwards) and after assimilating the subtle energies of the sun enter the body of the seeker. Due to the effect of these powers, not only the diseases of the body but also the diseases of the brain are also removed.

In modern language, the Vedic system of medicine is called the ceremonial-religious-medicinal medical system i.e. magic religious-medical treatment system.

On February 13, 2018, in Dainik Jagran published from New Delhi, light is being thrown on the topic of mantra therapy by taking the intent of a report by journalist Atul Pataria.

Swami Niranjananand Saraswati says that the science of mantra is also at the centre of research. The energy generated by the mental and external recitation of each mantra has been measured by a special type of quantum machine. This science has been the subject of Indian Yoga Science. Efforts are being made to understand the operation and transmission of mental energy on a scientific basis.

It is further told that the energy generated during the mental and external recitation of various mantras was measured through the quantum machine and this research machine, which is a unique instrument of science, has been brought to the Yoga Research Center in Bihar, Munger. When the Mahamrityunjaya Mantra was recited in front of this yantra, so much energy was generated that the thorn of the meter in the yantra kept on fluttering till it reached the last point.

Dena Jackson, a graduate student of the California College of Ayurveda, has written an article on sound therapy which is available on the website "Sounds of Healing". In this, the opinion of Dena Jackson is also similar to that of Swami Niranjanand. Out of the different mantras of Rigveda, she takes Gayatri Mantra and Mahamrityunjaya Mantra prominently. In fact all the sounds of all mantras, Pranayama originates from the sound "Om".

According to researchers from Ohio University in the US, when the effect of the mantras of Samaveda and the recitation of Hanuman Chalisa on the lining of cancerous lungs, intestine, brain, breast, skin and fibroblasts, there was a significant decline in the growth of cancer cells. In contrast, fast-paced western music and loud rock music were found to increase cancer cells.

In mantra therapy, clinical trials were conducted on 5000 people of about 50 diseases.

In which 70% of respiratory diseases like asthma.

60% in skin and anxiety related diseases.

55% in people with high blood pressure and hypertension.

51% in Arthritis Joint Pain.

34% in visual conditions.

The benefit was seen till now. Certainly, mantra therapy is a boon for those people who are suffering from chronic and chronic diseases.

German scientists say that when a person speaks something with his mouth, then his voice vibrates, which are about 175 types. Like the cuckoo sings in the fifth voice. His voice has about 500 types of vibrations. If Gayatri Mantra is felt in different instruments, then about 700 types of vibrations are felt. German scientists also say that if a person does not recite, but only listens, then he also has an effect.

The mantra is described in the name of Dev Vivaya Sarya because in Ayurveda and it has been written that its use is described in the name of spiritual therapy like blessings, God's grace, mangal, gift, home, rule, atonement, fasting etc. It is used in the treatment of various diseases. This is called "Sattva Bhagya".

The effect of the mantra is on the body, the mind, and also the soul. Due to this, various types of chemical and physical changes are visible inside the body. The toxicity of brain and cells can be removed by mantra.

Solo singing or group singing of Veda Mantras destroys diseases, similar to classical singing or other types of music. A 2010 study published in the Journal of Alzheimer's Disease by the Alzheimer's Research and Prevention Foundation as well as the University of Pennsylvania reviewed a group of patients with brain problems with numerical testing and memory. They were instructed to practice Kirtan Kriya for 12 minutes a day. Those patients chanted the name of Ram with singing and also chanted Om in singing.

In addition, another group practiced meditation for 12 minutes. Also, a third group listened to a Mozart violin concerto for 12 minutes.

Now after 15 days, this effect was found in these three groups that the blood effect in the brain of the Kirtan group was found to be increased. Whereas in the meditation group it was found to be slightly less. The other third group that listened to Mozart's violin concerts showed non-significant growth in different areas of the brain.

In 2010, a study was conducted at Parimala Hospital in Bangalore, India, which examined the effect of chanting on neck pain. The participants were trained in the 'Yogic Mind Sound Resonance Technique (MSRT), which included mantras such as Om and Mahamrityunjaya. Participants were given conventional physiotherapy for 30 minutes followed by MSRT for 20 minutes. After this full 50-minute period, the study group had significantly better results in pain lining, tenderness, neck flexion, and anxiety.

Disease prevention by vedic mantras

In Agra Saturday, 09 May 2020 – News - The effect of the mantra was published in Dainik Jagran by Tanu Gupta. On the occasion of National Prayer Day in America, President Donald Trump invited a Hindu priest to the White House to make peace lessons to the Vedic mantras which are given prominence in Sanatan Dharma. Mantras of Shanti Path (lesson chant) were recited for the safety and health of everyone affected by Corona.

As per Dr. Joshi of Ujjain's Dharma Vigyan Shodh Sansthan and religious scientist Pandit Vaibhav Joshi, who researched the topic of health-related to mantra. Dr. Joshi told Jagran.com that there is a direct path (lesson) to cleanliness and purity of body and mind, and the power of mantra can also bring alive the waning power of life.

According to Dr. Joshi, in religious and spiritual traditions around the world, the sound is considered important in creating, maintaining, and nurturing the universe. The belief that vibration permeates all visible and invisible things has been the scientific basis of music therapy.

For example, people like Ojha, Neel, Membo, Jhankari and Shaman have been doing indigenous therapy with music for a long time and they are psychologists and physicians in a way. They use sound as the main means of awakening the inner consciousness, relieving pain, and reaching the highest. Sound has an effect on nature, animals, and humans alike.

Diagnosis of diseases by mantras in Arthavaveda

According to religious scientist Pandit Vaibhav Joshi, many unique secrets have been told in Atharvaveda, including disease diagnosis, tantra-mantra sadhana through mantras. In the Vedic period, by the practice of Veda Mantras, examples of healing, and spiritual progress of many patients are found. This point has been proved many times by scholars like Mahabhashyakar Patanjali, Veda Bhashyakar Sayan, etc. In the first part of Atharvaveda, chanting and meditation have been given for healing from some specific mantras.

Contact

9839093003

myrichindia@gmail.com

facebook.com/drjagadeeshpillaiofficial

youtube.com/drjagadeeshpillai

|| lLOKAHA SAMSTHAHA SUKHINO BHAVANTU ||

• 39 •